Canada

by Shirley W. Gray

Content Adviser: Professor Sherry L. Field,
Department of Social Science Education, College of Education,
The University of Georgia

Reading Adviser: Dr. Linda D. Labbo,
Department of Reading Education, College of Education,
The University of Georgia

COMPASS POINT BOOKS

Minneapolis, Minnesota

FIRST REPORTS

Compass Point Books
3109 West 50th Street, #115
Minneapolis, MN 55410

Visit Compass Point Books on the Internet at *www.compasspointbooks.com* or e-mail your
request to *custserv@compasspointbooks.com*

Photographs ©:
David Falconer, cover; Unicorn Stock Photos/Aneal Vohra, 4; Photo Network/Nancy Hoyt Belcher, 6; Photo Network/
Bill Terry, 7; Tom Stack and Associates/Thomas Kitchin, 8, 9; James P. Rowan, 10; Index Stock Imagery, 11, 12; Tom Stack
and Associates/Thomas Kitchin, 13; Visuals Unlimited/Larry Blank, 14; Robert McCaw, 15; Photri-Microstock, 16; Tom Stack
and Associates/Thomas Kitchin, 17; Visuals Unlimited/Glenn Oliver, 18; Tom Stack and Associates/John Shaw, 19; Photophile,
20; Internatinal Stock/C. Bonington, 21; Corbis, 22; North Wind Picture Archives, 24, 25; Archive Photos, 26; North Wind
Picture Archives, 27; Tom Stack and Associates/Thomas Kitchin, 28, 29; Corbis/Leonard de Selva, 30; North Wind Picture
Archives, 31; Photo Network/Nancy Hoyt Belcher, 32; Tom Stack and Associates/Victoria Hurst, 34; Winston Fraser, 35;
Tom Stack and Associates/Thomas Kitchin, 36; Photophile, 37; Visuals Unlimited/Bill Banaszewski, 38; Winston Fraser,
39; Visuals Unlimited/George Herben, 40; Visuals Unlimited/Tim Hauf, 41; Index Stock Imagery/Yvette Cardozo, 42;
Trip/N. Price, 43; StockHaus Ltd., 45 top; Unicorn Stock Photos/Jim Shippee, 45 bottom.

Editors: E. Russell Primm and Emily J. Dolbear
Photo Researcher: Svetlana Zhurkina
Photo Selector: Dawn Friedman
Design: Bradfordesign, Inc.
Cartography: XNR Productions, Inc.

Library of Congress Cataloging-in-Publication Data

Gray, Shirley W.
  Canada / by Shirley W. Gray.
      p. cm. — (First reports)
   Includes bibliographical references and index.
   Summary: An introduction to the geography, history, culture, and people of Canada.
   ISBN 0-7565-0028-1 (hardcover)
   ISBN 0-7565-1202-6 (paperback)
      1. Canada—Juvenile literature. [1. Canada.] I. Title. II. Series.
   F1008.2 .G73 2000
   971—dc21   00-008556

Table of Contents

O Canada!

▲ *A member of the Royal Canadian Mounted Police*

"*Bonjour!* Good day! Welcome to Canada!"

You might hear this greeting if you visit Canada. Canada is the most northern country in North America. It is also the second-largest country in the world. Only Russia has more land.

▲ Map of Canada

Canada's neighbor to the south is the United States. Its neighbor to the northwest is also the United States—Alaska. To the north is the country of Greenland. Canada also touches three oceans. The Atlantic Ocean is on the east, and the Pacific Ocean is on the west, and the Arctic Ocean is to the north.

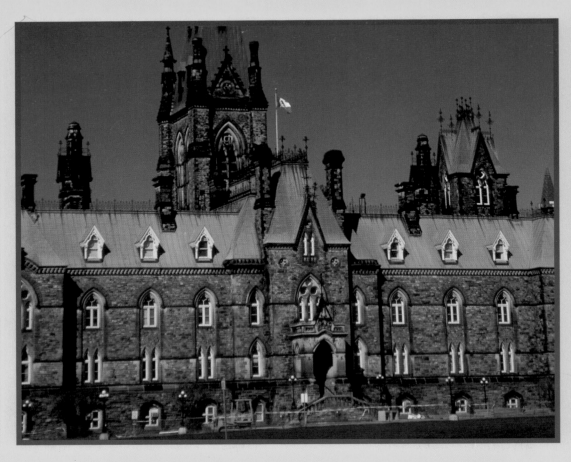

▲ *Parliament Hill is in Ottawa, the capital city of Canada.*

Northern Canada almost reaches the North Pole.

Canada has ten **provinces** and three **territories**. The capital city of Canada is Ottawa. Ottawa stands in the province of Ontario. It is less than one hour north of the United States by car.

Land and Water in Canada

Canada's land is varied. It has low valleys, high mountains, and vast areas of flat land called **plains**. They are in the middle of the country. Canada has many islands near its coasts. One of these is Prince Edward Island. This island is about the size of the U.S. state of Delaware. Newfoundland is also an island. It's the newest province. It joined Canada in 1949. Only Prince Edward Island has fewer people than Newfoundland.

▲ *A lighthouse on Prince Edward Island*

▲ *Canada is full of lakes, such as Moraine Lake in Banff National Park.*

Water is also an important part of Canada.
The nation has more lakes and water than any other
country in the world.

Most Canadians live on the flat plains near the
Saint Lawrence River. This important river connects

▲ The busy port of Quebec City on the Saint Lawrence River

the Great Lakes to the Atlantic Ocean. Workers made the river deep enough for huge ocean ships to sail on. Now ocean-going ships can carry goods to large inland cities such as Montreal. Large ships from around the world can now travel to such cities as Chicago.

▲ *Lake Ontario is one of the Great Lakes.*

Lake Ontario is one of the five Great Lakes of North America. It lies at the head of the Saint Lawrence River. The land near the lake has very rich soil. Farm crops and forests thrive here.

▲ *Maple trees are a familiar sight in Canada.*

One popular tree in Canada is the maple tree. This kind of tree loses its leaves every year. The maple leaf is Canada's national symbol. It was included on Canada's new flag in 1965.

Flatlands and Highlands

▲ *A prairie in Saskatchewan*

The Central Plains are a vast area of flat grassland in the center of Canada. When French explorers first saw it, they called it a **prairie**. *Prairie* is a French word that means "meadow." Herds of buffalo, deer, elk, and moose once fed on the grasses there. Now farmers

▲ *The Appalachian Mountains in Quebec*

grow wheat, barley, rye, and oats on the plains.

Two mountain ranges that begin in the United States cross into Canada. In the east are the Appalachian Mountains. This part of Canada looks like the U.S. states of Vermont and Maine. Farmers grow their crops in the valleys.

▲ *The Canadian Rocky Mountains stretch between the United States and Canada.*

In the west, the Rocky Mountains stretch from the United States into northern Alaska. Some mountains in the Rockies are the highest in North America. Snow and ice cover them all year round.

Many of the people in this region live in small mining towns. Silver, lead, and coal are found in the mountains.

The Canadian Shield and Tundra

The largest part of Canada is called the Canadian Shield. Millions of years ago, **glaciers** scraped away much of the soil in this area. Glaciers are huge sheets of ice that move slowly over the land. The glaciers dug out deep lakes and left rocks on the ground.

▲ *A lake in the Canadian Shield in northern Ontario*

▲ *This glacier is in Jasper National Park in Alberta.*

▲ *The Arctic tundra in the Northwest Territories*

In the north, the ground is frozen most of the year. For a few weeks in the summer, the ground thaws enough to let moss, grass, wild flowers, and small bushes grow. But trees cannot grow here. This land is called the **tundra**.

▲ *Two caribou graze on the tundra.*

Caribou—a kind of deer—feed off the small plants that grow on the tundra. Many animals live on the Canadian tundra. Wolves, snowy owls, and Artic foxes are among the most plentiful species.

▲ *Polar bears also live on the Canadian tundra.*

Polar bears live here too. They catch fish on the lakes through holes in the ice. In late November or early December, the female polar bears usually give birth to twin cubs. Polar bear families stay together for about two years.

▲ A totem pole carved by Canada's Native Americans.

The Native People of Canada

The first people to live in Canada probably came from Asia thousands of years ago. Most of these early people were hunters. They used animals for food and clothing. They ate caribou and bison, or buffalo. They wore the thick fur of bears, beavers, and other animals to keep warm.

▲ *Native Americans called Inuit travel with their dogs.*

▲ *Canada gets its name from the Iroquois people.*

Native Americans who spoke similar languages formed groups called nations. The nations of the Huron and the Iroquois lived in the lowlands near the Saint Lawrence River. The name *Canada* came from an Iroquois word meaning "village" or "community."

The Inuit, a group of Native Americans in the north, lived on the tundra. They survived the hard weather by hunting seals and caribou. Inuit still live on the tundra today.

European Explorers

▲ *Norwegian pirates called Vikings traveled by sea to the Canadian coast.*

The first Europeans probably visited Canada in the year 1000. Leif Eriksson and his group of Norwegian pirates called Vikings may have settled on the North Atlantic coast. Hundreds of years later, French, English, and Dutch sailors explored Canada.

▲ *Europeans traded furs with Native Americans.*

Some Native Americans helped the Europeans. They taught them how to fish and trap animals. Sadly, the Europeans wanted all the land for themselves. They forced the Native Americans out of their hunting grounds. They also brought European diseases.

▲ *Samuel de Champlain*

In 1608, a French explorer named Samuel de Champlain started a small trading fort on the Saint Lawrence River. The Native Americans traded beaver fur with the French for tools and other supplies. The French took over this area and called it New France.

▲ *A Hudson's Bay Company trading store*

Soon the English explorers opened trading posts too. The English started the Hudson's Bay Company in 1670. The English controlled settlements along the Atlantic Coast. The French controlled those along the Saint Lawrence River.

▲ Chateau Frontenac is a famous castle hotel in Quebec City.

The French and English fought for many years in Europe and in North America. Each country wanted more land. Finally, in 1763, the English took control of New France.

The English could not make the people in New France give up their language or culture though. In 1791, Quebec was divided into two colonies. Upper Canada was English and later became Ontario. Lower Canada remained French. Today most people who live in Quebec City come from French families. They prefer to speak and write French.

▲ *Signs in Quebec are written in French.*

Settling the West

▲ *An early settler's log hut in the Canadian wilderness*

Fur traders started moving farther west into central Canada. Many of them married Native American women. These families stayed on the frontier. They were called Métis. The name comes from a French word that means "mixed."

▲ *The Hudson's Bay Company sold supplies to gold seekers.*

Other people began moving west too. Some came from the United States. Many tried farming or ranching in the Central Plains. In the 1850s, gold was discovered in the province of British Columbia. People rushed west hoping to strike it rich.

▲ *Two members of today's Royal Canadian Mounted Police in their bright red uniforms*

White settlers took land from the Native Americans. Many times they mistreated or fought the Indians. The Native Americans demanded that the Canadian government protect them. The government created a police force called the Royal Canadian Mounted Police. The Mounted Police wore bright red coats, rode horses, and carried guns. Canada still has this group of police officers today.

Canada Today

▲ The changing of the guard in Ottawa is a popular British tradition.

Canada gained control of its own government in 1982. It still has ties to Britain, however. The king or queen of Britain is the official head of Canada but has no real power. In Canada, the prime minister is in charge of the government. He or she is elected by the people.

▲ *A fiddling contest on Canada Day in Quebec*

Canadians are free to worship as they choose. Most people in Canada are Christian and celebrate holidays such as Christmas and Easter. Canada Day— July 1 is a national holiday. On this day, everyone celebrates Canada's birthday with fireworks and picnics.

▲ The skyline of Vancouver, British Columbia

More than 29 million people live in Canada today. That's about the same number of people who live in California! Many people live near the U.S. border. The largest cities in Canada are Toronto, Montreal, Vancouver, and Calgary.

▲ *Canada has residents from many countries, including China.*

The first **immigrants** were French and English. Many of their relatives still live in Canada today. However, Canada also has many immigrants from around the world. Canada now includes people from countries in Asia and Europe.

Sports

Winter usually lasts longer than summer in Canada. But Canadians know how to have fun, even in cold weather. Canadians created the sport of ice hockey in 1875. It is now played around the world. Ice hockey is one of the most exciting events in the Winter Olympics every four years.

Ice-skating, cross-country skiing, and downhill skiing are also popular. Many children go to indoor skating rinks before school to practice ice-skating and hockey.

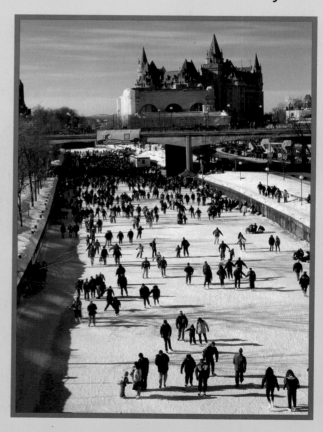

▲ Ice skaters flock to the frozen Rideau Canal in Ottawa.

▲ *Professional ice hockey is very popular in Canada.*

▲ *Canadians enjoy hiking in the country's many national parks*

National and provincial parks protect large wilderness areas in Canada. Here Canadians can enjoy hiking, camping, and fishing—in summer and winter. The parks are in all the provinces of this huge country.

▲ *Ice fishing in Manitoba*

When the lakes are frozen, fishers cut holes in the ice and drop their lines into the water. The lakes are dotted with small wooden huts. Inside the huts, fishers try to stay warm while they fish.

Life in the Tundra

▲ *A couple in Nunavut*

In 1999, part of the Northwest Territories was made into a new territory. The new territory is called Nunavut. *Nunavut* means "our land" in the language of the Inuit. More than three-fourths of the people who live in Nunavut are Inuit.

Most Inuit children speak their native language—Inukitut. They also learn English in school. Some Inuit children use the Internet to share stories about Arctic life with schoolchildren in other parts of the world.

Thousands of people visit various parts of Canada each year. If you visit, you will learn more interesting facts about this large country. Then as you leave, you will probably say, "*Merci beaucoup!* Thank you very much. I enjoyed my visit to Canada."

▲ *Inuit students in school*

Glossary

glaciers—huge sheets of ice that move slowly

immigrants—people who come to a foreign country to live

plains—flat land

prairie—grasslands

provinces—areas of land in Canada that are a political unit

territories—areas of land in Canada that are not officially provinces

tundra—treeless land in the north where the ground stays frozen most of the year

Did You Know?

- Nunavut is the largest Canadian territory. It covers three time zones.

- Quebec has two separate school systems—one for French speakers and one for English speakers.

- Wayne Gretzky first went skating when he was two years old. He loved it so much that his father made a backyard ice rink for him to practice hockey.

Official name: Canada

Capital: Ottawa, Ontario

Official language(s): English and French

National song: "O Canada"

Area: 3,849,674 square miles (9,970,610 square kilometers)

Highest point: Mount Logan, 19,524 feet (5,951 meters)

Lowest point: Sea level

Population: 29,450,000 (1998 estimate)

Head of government: Prime minister

Money: Canadian dollar

Important Dates

1000   Leif Eriksson and Vikings explore the coast of Newfoundland.

1608   French explorer Samuel de Champlain starts a trading fort on the St. Lawrence River.

1670   The English starts the Hudson Bay Trading Company.

1763   The English take control of New France.

1791   Quebec is divided into Upper Canada and Lower Canada.

1850s   Gold is discovered in the province of British Columbia.

1875   Canadians create the sport of ice hockey.

1982   Canada gains control of its own government.

1999   Part of the Northwest Territories become the new territory of Nunavut.

At the Library

Bryant, Adam. *Canada, Good Neighbor to the World*. Parsippany, N.J.: Dillon Press, 1997.

Greenwood, Barbara. *The Kids Book of Canada*. Buffalo, N.Y.: Kids Can Press, 1998.

Kalman, Bobbie, and Niki Walker. *Canada from A to Z*. New York: Crabtree Pub. Co., 1999.

Lye, Keith. *Take a Trip to Canada*. New York: Franklin Watts, 1983.

On the Web

For more information on *Canada,* use FactHound to track down Web sites related to this book.

1. Go to *www.facthound.com*
2. Type in a search word related to this book or this book ID: 0756500281.
3. Click on the *Fetch It* button.

Your trusty FactHound will fetch the best Web sites for you!

Through the Mail

Embassy of Canada
501 Pennsylvania Avenue, N.W.
Washington, DC 20001
For information about the country

On the Road

Canadian Tourism Commission
8th Floor West, 235 Queen Street
Ottawa, Ontario
K1A 0H6 Canada
613/946-1000
To find out about visiting Canada

About the Author

Shirley W. Gray received her bachelor's degree in education from the University of Mississippi and her master's degree in technical writing from the University of Arkansas. She teaches writing and works as a scientific writer and editor. Shirley W. Gray lives with her husband and two sons in Little Rock, Arkansas.